MASTER THIS!

Gymnastics

Tracey Royle

WAKEFIELD LIBRARIES

Printed by Wayland in 2012.

Hachette Children's Books
338 Euston Road
London NW1 3BH

Wayland Australia
Level 17/207 Kent Street
Sydney NSW 2000

Commissioning editor: Jennifer Sanderson
Senior editor: Claire Shanahan
Produced by Tall Tree Ltd
Editor, Tall Tree: Jon Richards
Designer: Ed Simkins

British Library Cataloguing in Publication Data
 Royle, Tracey.
   Gymnastics. -- (Master this)
   1. Gymnastics--Juvenile literature.
   I. Title II. Series
   796.4'42-dc22

ISBN: 9780750268202

First published in 2009 by Wayland
Copyright © Wayland 2009
This paperback edition printed by Wayland in 2012

Printed in China

Wayland is a division of Hachette Children's Books,
an Hachette UK company.
www.hachette.co.uk

Picture credits
All photographs taken by Michael Wicks, except:
t-top, b-bottom, l-left, r-right, c-centre
Cover Dreamstime.com/Julia Taranova,
4 Dreamstime.com/Grosremy, 5 Dreamstime.com/Valeria
Cantone, 13t Jamie Lantzy, 14t Wally McNamee/Corbis
14b Dreamstime.com/Shariff Che' Lah, 17t Wally
McNamee/Corbis, 27t Frank May/epa/Corbis,
29l Dreamstime.com/Grosremy

The website addresses (URLs) included in this book were
valid at the time of going to press. However, because of
the nature of the Internet, it is possible that some
addresses may have changed, or sites may have changed
or closed down since publication. While the author and
publisher regret any inconvenience this may cause the
readers, no responsibility for any such changes can be
accepted by either the author or the publisher.

Disclaimer
In preparation of this book, all due care has been
exercised with regard to the advice, activities and
techniques depicted. The publishers regret that they can
accept no liability for any loss or injury sustained. When
learning a new sport it is important to get expert tuition
and to follow a manufacturer's instructions.

Acknowledgements
The author and publisher would like to thank the
following for their help and participation in this book:
Marriotts Gymnastics Club, Sophie Cripps,
Daniel Gardner, Jack Maydom, Mollie Smith
and Lauren Doherty

Contents

In the gym

Gymnastics is an exciting sport that combines agility, strength and timing to create breathtaking displays on various pieces of equipment, such as the floor, beam and vault.

Early gymnastics

People have been performing gymnastic exercises for thousands of years. The earliest male gymnasts performed naked, while women were banned from taking part. Gymnastics appeared at the Olympic Games in Athens in 1896. Rhythmic gymnastics (see pages 14–15) was first recognised in 1962 and appeared at the Olympics for the first time in 1996.

Diet

Gymnasts need to stay fit and healthy to perform at their peak. Eating the right foods is vital to keeping their bodies in shape. A healthy diet should include plenty of fresh fruit and vegetables and be low in fat. It should also have foods that contain lots of protein, such as chicken and beans, to help build muscles, and carbohydrates, such as pasta, to give you energy.

This gymnast is performing on a piece of apparatus called a pommel. His routine includes swinging his legs and body around the pommel, while holding onto the handles in the middle.

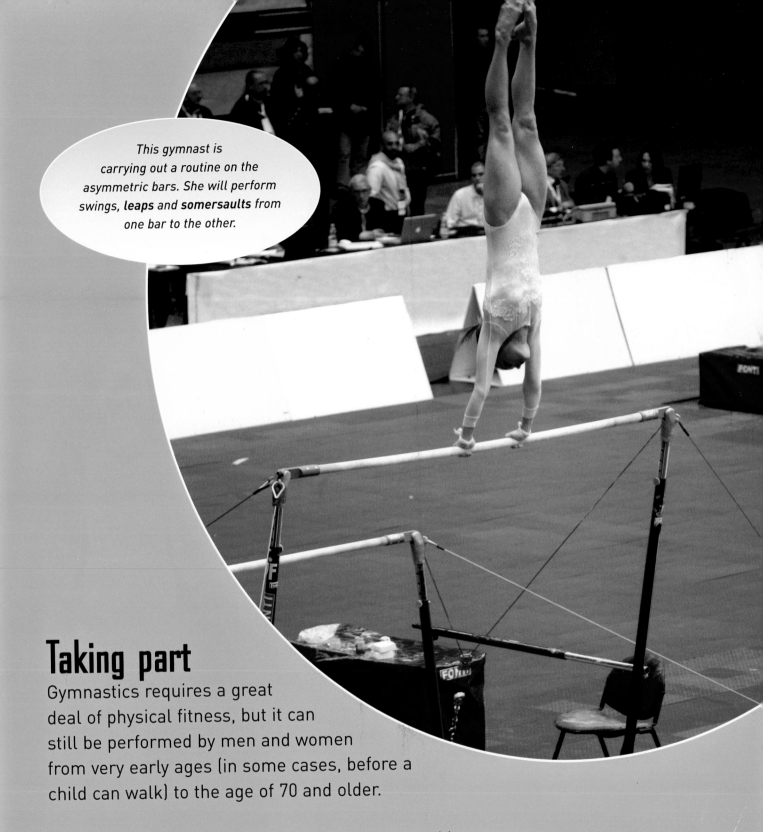

This gymnast is carrying out a routine on the asymmetric bars. She will perform swings, *leaps* and **somersaults** from one bar to the other.

Taking part

Gymnastics requires a great deal of physical fitness, but it can still be performed by men and women from very early ages (in some cases, before a child can walk) to the age of 70 and older.

However, not all of the disciplines are performed by everyone. Men and women perform on the floor and the vault, while only women perform on the beam and the asymmetric bars. Men perform on the pommel horse, the rings, the **parallel** bars and the high bar.

Clothing and kit

Clothing for gymnasts is quite simple. It should be close-fitting so that it does not get in the way, but not so tight that it restricts your movement. Other personal equipment includes hand grips and chalk.

What to wear

Girls train in **leotards** and occasionally gym shorts, while boys wear a leotard or a T-shirt and shorts. In competition, girls wear a leotard with either long or short sleeves. For rhythmic gymnastics (see pages 14–15), the leotards can be decorated with diamanté and sequins. Boys wear a leotard and shorts during competition floor exercises and the vault. They wear long trousers with stirrups (hoops at the bottom of each leg to go around the feet) and socks when competing on the other apparatus.

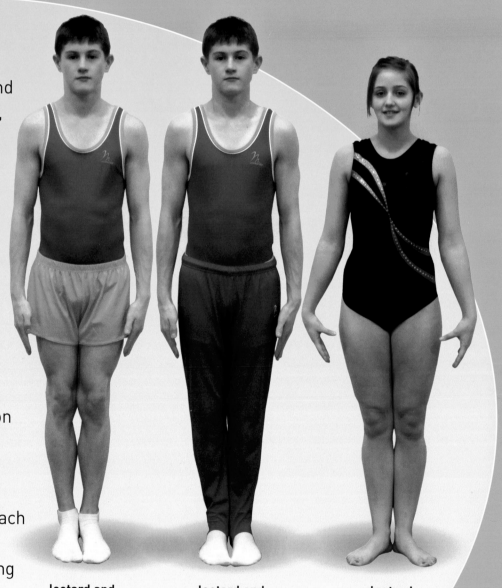

leotard and shorts

leotard and long trousers

leotard

Grips and chalk

Gymnasts wear hand grips during displays on the bars and rings. These are not compulsory, but they prevent the hands from ripping or tearing, which can occur during many hours of training. Men's hand grips are different from women's as men hold the bars and rings differently. Both men's and women's hand grips are caked in chalk (magnesium) using water or a spray.

Hand grips

A man's hand grip has three finger holes to hook over the middle three fingers.

A woman's hand grip has two finger holes and is thinner than a man's. Young male gymnasts sometimes use these grips.

Chalking up

Solid blocks of chalk are rubbed onto hand grips to cover them.

Loose chalk powder is rubbed onto the hands when hand grips are not used.

Top tip

You should never wear jewellery while doing gymnastics. Not only is it dangerous, but you will also be penalised if you wear jewellery during a competition. You should always tie back your hair so that it is not in your eyes.

Shapes and conditioning

Gymnastics is a very active sport and you should make sure that you are physically fit enough to take part. Your coach can show you several positions, called 'shapes', and exercises to improve your fitness.

Gymnastic shapes

Different shapes will help you train for different disciplines. You should concentrate on getting the positions correct and holding them for several seconds. Doing this will exercise specific muscles and improve your technique for different disciplines.

The back support helps to develop body posture for parallel bars and the pommel.

The front support is helpful for improving skills for the parallel bars and the pommel.

The arch is good at developing swinging and **tumbling** techniques.

The dish helps to improve strength and techniques for swings and tumbles.

The **pike** shape is important for rotational, or turning, skills used in vaulting.

The tuck is helpful in developing tumbling skills.

Conditioning exercises

As well as shapes, there are several active exercises that can be used to improve technique and strength even further. These should be attempted only after the shapes have been mastered. For example, press-ups are taught after the basic front support shape has been perfected.

Press-ups

Basic press-ups are performed with the elbows held in. The gymnast lowers herself slowly until her nose touches the floor and then pushes herself up.

For an advanced press-up, the legs are lifted until the gymnast is pushing up from a **handstand** position. This develops arm and shoulder strength.

Sit-ups

Basic sit-ups (left) are performed with the feet under a wall bar before they are taken to an advanced level (see below).

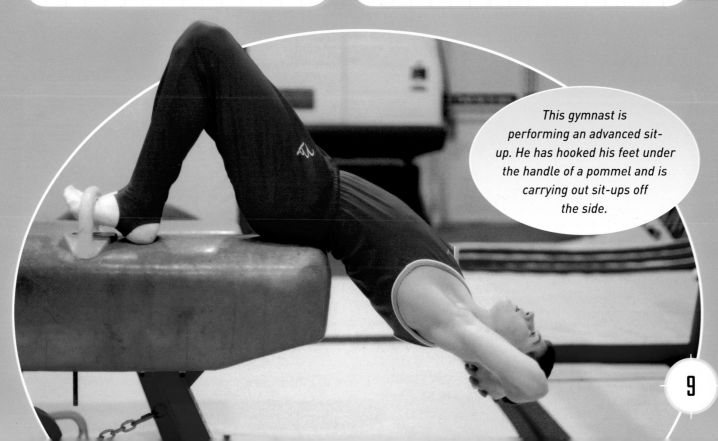

This gymnast is performing an advanced sit-up. He has hooked his feet under the handle of a pommel and is carrying out sit-ups off the side.

The floor

The floor features some of the most breathtaking gymnastic performances, where male and female gymnasts demonstrate power, strength and grace in a series of simple moves and complicated tumbles.

Top tip

You can learn rolls correctly by performing them on a padded slope. This will make turning easier, allowing you to concentrate on getting the right technique.

Basic skills

The first floor skills learned are rolls, which can be forwards, backwards or sideways. Once basic rolls have been mastered, they can be developed into more advanced skills, such as handstand forwards rolls, **dive rolls** and somersaults.

The handstand is another important floor skill and it can also be used for other apparatus, such as the bars, beam and vault. The last important skill is the **cartwheel**, which is developed when learning how to tumble.

Forwards roll

1. The gymnast starts in a squat with her arms held out in front of her.

2. She puts her hands on the floor and rolls onto her back.

3. She lands on the balls of her feet and pushes herself upright.

In or out?

The edge of the floor is marked by a thick border – gymnasts cannot touch or go outside this border during a routine, otherwise they will be penalised.

in

out

Floor competition

Both males and females compete on the floor. Females perform a routine lasting no more than 90 seconds, while men have a maximum of 70 seconds. These routines should contain tumbles, leaps, spins and jumps. Females' routines are performed to music.

This gymnast is performing a cartwheel. She keeps her legs wide apart to complete the move as smoothly as possible.

Straddle press to handstand

1

The gymnast places his feet wide apart and leans forwards.

2

He puts his hands shoulder width apart and raises his legs.

3

He brings his legs together to form a handstand.

Parallel and high bars

These male disciplines are both performed on bars, but the skills required for them are very different. Performing on the high bar involves building swings into releases and **catches**, while the parallel bars involve swings, turns and twists between the bars.

The parallel bars

The gymnast has to mount the 2-metre-high parallel bars on his own, although he may use a springboard to do so. The two bars are between 42 centimetres and 52 centimetres apart and gymnasts use them to perform routines that include handstands, somersaults, turns and **holds**, before finally dismounting to one side.

Swing to handstand

1	2	3
The gymnast starts to bring his legs forwards.	He then begins to swing his legs back with enough force to lift his body behind him.	At the top of the swing, he needs to work hard to hold the handstand.

The high bar

The bar is made of metal and is 2.55 metres above the ground. The routines are similar to those performed on the asymmetric bars, and include swings, turns, somersaults, releases and dismounts. During training, these moves are practised over a large pit that is filled with foam to protect you should you fall.

This gymnast is being lifted onto the high bar by his coach at the start of a routine.

Giant swing with twist

The gymnast maintains a firm body position at the top of his swing.

At the bottom, he bends slightly so that his feet lead the upwards swing.

To perform a twist, the gymnast lets go with one hand at the top of a swing. He spins his body around 180 degrees to face in the opposite direction. He changes from a forwards to a reverse grip.

Top tip

Your training routine should include the dish and arch shapes (see pages 8–9). These are helpful in conditioning your body and perfecting the techniques needed to perform swings on both the parallel and high bars.

23

The rings

This piece of apparatus shows the strength, flexibility and control of male gymnasts as they perform acrobatic swings and powerful holds while suspended 2.75 metres above the floor.

wooden dowel

The hand grips used on the rings have pieces of dowel, or small wooden rods, in them. These rods are inserted into loops in the hand grips just under the tips of the fingers. As the gymnast's fingers wrap around the rings, these dowels help him to grip the rings.

This gymnast is performing an L hold. During a competition, he has to keep still in this hold for at least two seconds, otherwise he will be penalised.

Holds

To perform a hold well, the gymnast needs to be stationary for a number of seconds. The L hold sees the gymnast's body and legs form an 'L' shape. For the iron cross, the gymnast holds his arms out straight to the sides at shoulder height while suspending his body. This is a difficult move and requires a lot of upper body strength. In the Maltese cross, the gymnast holds his body parallel to the floor at ring height.

Swings

The giant swings performed on the rings are similar to those performed on the high bar. The gymnast swings from one handstand to another with his arms extended. Other moves that are performed during a competition routine are a swing to a handstand, a dismount and a hold.

Top tip

During a routine, you should always look to keep the ropes holding the rings tight. If the ropes go slack at any point, you could be hurt as the rings will jar with each swing.

This gymnast is performing a dismount. He has built up enough momentum for him to perform a somersault after releasing the rings and then land on both feet.

Swing

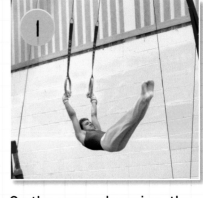

On the upwards swing, the gymnast's body bends, so the feet are raised high.

Towards the top of the swing, the gymnast's body straightens out.

His body arches slightly during the downwards swing.

25

The pommel

Pommel is one of the hardest male gymnastic disciplines as it requires strength over the whole body. The arms and upper body have to support you, while the legs and stomach keep your body rigid during circles, **flares** and dismounts.

Getting on and off

As with the parallel bars, the gymnast mounts without any help. Dismounting is usually to a landing mat that is placed to one side.

Pommel is practised on a mushroom. This is closer to the ground than a pommel, so there is less chance of injury when practising moves such as flares.

The routine

Each routine should be continuous, without the gymnast stalling or falling off. It should include double leg circles, where the gymnast spins around the pommel with both legs held together, and flares, where the legs are wide apart during the spin. Also included are scissors, where the legs straddle either side of the pommel, and swings up to handstands.

Star file

LOUIS SMITH
Rising star

Louis Smith became the first British gymnast to win an Olympic medal since 1928, when he earned the bronze on the pommel at the 2008 Beijing Games. Previously, Smith had won the Commonwealth gold medal in 2006 and a bronze at the World Championships in 2007.

Double leg circles

1

With both hands on the handles, the gymnast swings his legs together.

2

With his back straight, his legs are brought in front of his body.

3

He raises his left hand and puts his weight on his right as his legs pass beneath.

4

The legs now pass behind the gymnast as he completes a full circle.

To perform a dismount, this gymnast has swung up into a handstand, before landing on both feet beside the pommel.

Taking it further

Taking part in gymnastics can be very demanding and requires many hours of training. Your local club will be able to give you guidance and coaching to develop the skills you need.

Finding a club

Use the Internet to find a suitable gymnastics club near to where you live, and check out the websites of your local and national gymnastics organisations. Once you have joined a club, you will have the chance to enter competitions at different levels, from local to regional, and maybe even to international level.

Top tip

Check that the coaches at the gymnastics club you want to join have the correct qualifications. You can check these out by looking at the website of your national gymnastics organisation.

A good gymnastics club will have a complete range of full-size equipment, as well as training and safety apparatus so that you can develop and practise your techniques.

Competition

Gymnastic routines are overseen by a panel of judges that awards points to decide the winners. Gymnasts have a starting value of points, which is decided by the difficulty of techniques used in the routine. These starting points and the difficulty of various moves are laid out by the FIG (*Fédération Internationale de Gymnastique*), the organisation that oversees gymnastics around the world. Points are then deducted for mistakes made during the display, such as falls and stumbles.

Other gymnastic sports

Gymnastics techniques can be used in several sports, such as trampolining, which uses similar twists and somersaults. Diving also uses gymnastics skills, and many of the conditioning exercises, such as the pike (see pages 8–9), are used to teach the correct body positions during a dive.

A panel of judges studies a performance at the Men's European Team championships in 2008. At big competitions, such as the Olympics, there are nine judges for each piece of apparatus.

Glossary

artistic gymnastics gymnastics routines that are performed on various pieces of apparatus, such as the floor, the pommel and the bars.

cartwheel a move where gymnasts make a sideways spin of their whole body after putting their hands on the floor.

catches a move performed on the high bar and asymmetric bars where the gymnast catches hold of the bars, after letting go of them to perform another move in the air.

circles a move that sees the gymnast move his or her whole body in a circle around a piece of apparatus. Circles are performed on the parallel bars and the pommel.

dismounts a move where the gymnast lands with his or her feet on the floor after performing on a piece of apparatus, such as the beam, vault, bars, rings or pommel.

dive rolls when a gymnast jumps high in the air and then lands into a forwards roll.

flares a pommel move where the gymnast spins around with his legs wide open.

handstand a move where gymnasts lift their whole body off the floor while upside down.

hemp a plant with fibres that can be woven together to make hard-wearing cloth or rope.

holds a move where the gymnast remains still in a certain position for a number of seconds.

leaps moves where the gymnast jumps high into the air, taking off on one foot and landing on the other foot.

leotards tight-fitting outfits that cover the body from the shoulders to the tops of the legs.

momentum the combination of an object's weight and movement.

mounts the first skill in a routine performed on the beam, vault, bars, rings or pommel, when the gymnast gets onto the equipment.

parallel when two bars, or lines, are separated by an equal distance at every point.

pike a gymnastics position where the gymnast bends his or her body at the waist while keeping the legs straight.

releases a gymnastics move where the gymnast lets go of a piece of apparatus to perform another move, before catching hold of the apparatus again. Releases are performed on the high bar and the asymmetric bars.

somersaults moves where gymnasts spin head over heels in mid-air. Somersaults can be performed forwards and backwards.

tumbling acrobatic skills such as somersaults linked together along the floor, usually on a diagonal. Only the hands and the feet should touch the floor during a tumbling sequence.

unison when skills are performed at the same time by a group of gymnasts.

walkovers moves where gymnasts put their hands on the floor, lift their legs over their body, put their feet on the floor and stand upright.

Gymnastics organisations

There are many organisations around the world that oversee gymnastics at various levels, from regional up to international. Each discipline also has its own organisation giving specialist advice.

The FIG oversees gymnastics around the world, representing all disciplines, including artistic, rhythmic and trampoline.

British Gymnastics oversees gymnastics throughout the UK. It provides advice on courses, qualifications for coaching and finding your nearest gymnastics club.

The International Gymnastics Hall of Fame celebrates the sport's best athletes, as well as the others who have contributed to gymnastics, including coaches and judges.

Further reading

There are plenty of books available for the newcomer as well as the more experienced gymnast.

Know Your Sport: Gymnastics Gifford, Clive (Franklin Watts, 2008)
A Perfect 10 Higgins, Chris (Hodder Children's Books, 2008)

Websites

The Internet is a great place for information on techniques, advice and chatrooms where you can exchange training tips.

www.drillsandskills.com
A website with tips and advice on graded skills for each piece of apparatus.

www.tulsagymnastics.com
Contains advice for parents, coaches and gymnasts on training both in the gym and at home.

www.fig-gymnastics.com
The website of the FIG, which has the latest news from around the world and links for information on all aspects of gymnastics.

Index